# EMISSARY

## PAINTINGS AND JOURNEY OF

## HELEN PERRY THICKENS RITCHIE

*Emissary: Paintings and Journey of Helen Perry Thickens Ritchie*

ISBN: Softcover 978-1-955581-22-6

Copyright © 2021 by Helen Perry Thickens Ritchie

All rights reserved. No part of this book may be reproduced or transmitted in any form or by any means, electronic or mechanical, including photocopying, recording, or by any information storage and retrieval system, without permission in writing from the publisher.

**Parson's Porch Books** is an imprint of Parson's Porch & Company (PP&C) in Cleveland, Tennessee. PP&C is an innovative organization which raises money by publishing books of noted authors, representing all genres. Its face and voice is **David Russell Tullock.**

Parson's Porch & Company *turns books into bread & milk* by sharing its profits with the poor.

www.parsonsporch.com

# EMISSARY

## HELEN PERRY THICKENS RITCHIE

The Emissary – A messenger sent into enemy territory knowing he could be killed.  A channel.   A vessel.

We who love Jesus Christ are all emissaries sent into the world.

# Acknowledgments

Hearing, Seeing, Knowing and Understanding the heart of a person is a true gift in relationships. I am deeply thankful to our son, Captain Jim V. Ritchie, MD, who exhibits these gifts. Jim's love of God was shown as he graciously photographed many of my paintings to fulfill a longtime desire to share with others my walk with Jesus.

To our dear sister in Christ and beloved friend, Mary Hood Dorrill who has used her wonderful technical skills to organize and categorize my paintings, listen to the stories from my heart about each painting and transcribe them. Her relentless dedication to Jim and me, we cannot repay.

To Jim, my precious husband of 60 years in June, I acknowledge I would not be the person I am today to express myself freely, have courage and acceptance, if it were not for his unconditional love of Jesus.

I am thankful for my daughter, Anne Ritchie Young, my prayer warrior, who is a multitalented, gifted person and beautiful reflection of our Lord.

I appreciate our grandchildren's love and inspiration which motivated me in bringing this book of paintings to pass.

To Pastor Larry Wilson and Pastor Peter O'pata who prophesied over me that I would write inspirational books.

# INTRODUCTION

What is a dream? What is a vision, a revelation? What is a prophecy? What is being alive?

The world we live in is called physical. How many human beings realize and know we are spirit and we are flesh (body, mind, soul, spirit, heart)? The spiritual realm is going on as we live here on earth, day and night.

Each person has his/her own journey. The relationship with our creator, God, is individual and corporate. We are always in relationship, close or far away.

I know God is real. God is spirit. My journey with God, Yahweh, has been growing in understanding and deeper beliefs. Accepting Jesus, the Messiah, God's son and gift of life and receiving the Holy Spirit is an ongoing relationship as He reveals and guides me daily.

Many dream symbols appear in reality as seen in physical forms. Many people experience this. The paintings are a variety of observations and experiences throughout my life.

I love horses and have ridden most of my life. I love birds, wildlife, flowers and gardening. I love people. Seeing the soft lights, colors, shadows and details enrich each day. How can one be bored with so much to observe?

Listening to people's stories is a blessing to me. I paint portraits, getting to know them and watch their mannerisms.  Many times people desire portraits of deceased family members.  I like for them to stand beside me and tell me what they want different.  They paint through me.  They will be with the painting.  My desire is for them to enjoy the results.

One of my 43 year old students said she had never seen a sunset until taking art lessons.

The Lord God Almighty knew us before He created the earth and called us by name.  He knew our strengths, weaknesses, talents and gifts.  The people He puts in our path can be mentors to help our talents blossom.

My grandparents, parents, teachers, family and friends have all enriched my life.  Mother gave my two sisters and me pencils, paper, scissors and colors and we all became artists.  Painting and drawing is like breathing to me.  I see patterns, lights, shadows, color, size, depth, perspective - potential for paintings as I live my days.  I love this gift God has given me.

I hope and pray you will "see" and enjoy these paintings I share with you.

The Approach

18 x 24     Watercolor

The painting is of the male dove coming to roost. I love to study the anatomy and detail of the birds and feathers.

Charger

8 ½ x 11     Pen and Ink

Thoroughbred Horse

Cleopatra

8 ½ x 11     Pen and Ink

Arabian Mare

Generation in Paints

12 x 16     Watercolor

Paint horses in a pasture that I have watched throughout the years. I stopped and rubbed them, visited with them and smelled the wonderful smell of horses.

The Spirit and the Bride Say Come Lord Jesus

22 x 29 ½     Watercolor

In Stallburg, NY, a vision came to me in the morning time of snow that covered the earth that looked like lace. The Bride of Christ and Holy Spirit were looking down from above saying, "Come, Lord Jesus, come soon."   1979

Jesus and the Disciples

30 x 39     Watercolor

Many of Jesus' disciples were fishermen and loved good stories. Jesus and all 12 disciples are depicted in the painting talking and laughing. It is up to you as to identify who you see as Jesus and each disciple.

Michael Guardian Angel

9 x 12  Watercolor

The image of my guardian angel came to me – strong, powerful, protective, obedient unto the Spirit of Holiness. He knew Jesus personally – full of wisdom, truth, knowledge, understanding, discernment and an ultimate warrior.

Guardian Angel

8 ½ x 11     Watercolor

Guardian Angel comes in human forms at times to bring messages.

The Celebration

18 x 24   Watercolor

My guardian angel comes in different forms – bringing messages.  YOU AREN'T PERFECT BUT YOU ARE LOVED AND THAT LOVE OVERCOMES ALL IMPERFECTIONS. I heard people celebrating and speaking in other languages.

You Are My Gift To You

19x24   Watercolor

Twice that day in 1979, God told me He was my God and there was none other. He said, "You are my gift to you. You are like a basket of flowers. The basket of flowers has beautiful roses with velvet soft petals and fragrant smell but has thorns that tear the flesh. Some of the flowers are snapdragons, some daisies, and some violets. Some haven't opened yet and some are faded but you have to accept the whole basket as a gift from me. You are my gift to you. You can dance; you can sing; you can paint; you can write; you can speak; you can do many things and it is your challenge to use the gifts I have given you in life." God is saying to you "You are my gift to you!" Accept yourself as a gift from God with endless possibilities. Love one another.

The Gift of Jewels

24 x 48        Acrylic

You can look and not see. On a very frigid early morning looking out the east window, I was amazed to see the ground covered in sparkling jewels of many colors as the sunlight hit the frosted blades of grass. It was such a gift to see other than just white sparkles. My husband saw the jewel colors, too. God blesses us in many ways.

Rainbow of Promise on I-55

18 x 24    Watercolor

While driving home after a storm, I witnessed an awesome, brilliant, huge rainbow that landed in front of me on I-55. Traffic was backed up for ½ mile. No one wanted to leave but gradually moved forward. As we went through the color, we entered a pristine white light area of about 20-30 feet. Golden 6-8 inch balls were floating in the white area. This experience was shared by hundreds.

Shared Promises on I-55

48 x 60 Acrylic

The shared experience of the rainbow on I-55 was so extraordinary, I wanted to portray the rainbow enlarged.

Mirror Miracle

15 x 20     Watercolor

Driving Home the setting sun was a ball of fire reflected in the pond. I looked to the east and the harvest moon was rising. To paint the painting, the moon and sun could not be on the same side so I painted it as a mirror. One of the definitions of mirror is miracle.

The Cave of my Heart

30 x 40    Oil

As I prayed and sought to be with Jesus, I would go up the wooded area path to an open field.  Jesus would be there standing or sitting by a tree.   I would sit down with Him and we would talk or He talks and I listen.  One day, He took my hand and led me across the field to an open cave.  The inner path led down to two openings.  The one on the right was pure white light and to the left was a large oval cave with two columns and a bench.  On the walls were paintings and torches between them.  Jesus and I would sit and be together on the bench.  It is the cave of my heart.

More and More Gold

48 x 60    Oil

One day, I couldn't find Jesus at the field where we met. I went into the cave and there He was down beside the glowing stairs underneath. He said nothing but looked at me within, knowing all. He reached under the stairs and took out handfuls of golden nuggets – more and more and more gold nuggets he handed me. Then He looked at me again, silently, and handed me more and more and more golden nuggets. He gives precious moments of golden nuggets to all of us.

The Garden of My Heart<br>
36 x 48           Oil

I had never questioned what was through the other opening at the back of the cave – being dark. One day, He took me by the hand and led me to this opening. I wondered – as He stepped up the few stairs. All became light and opened into a beautiful garden like an atrium with sky, clouds, mist, and sunlight. He went and sat on the bench there beside the stream of Living Water. The animals and birds came to be with Him – Love, Peace, Joy, Life. "I am the way, the truth and the Life", Jesus said. This is where Jesus lives in the cave and garden of my heart.

The Armor of God

36 x 48    Oil

Driving home on Highway 16, I saw a vision of a man in armor walking on water and heard "the armor of God, helmet of salvation, shield of faith, breastplate of righteousness, sword of the Spirit - the Word, the belt of truth and shod with the gospel of peace".

Revelation to John

48 x 60        Oil

Paintings grow and develop as we create what is revealed. The number five means grace.

God the Father with a double-edged sword; Jesus, our Lord and Savior, the Lamb of God, the Lion of the tribe of Judah. He offers the bread and wine as His body and blood to all who receive Him. Jesus said the Holy Spirit, God the Father and He will come and live with us and within us. He will fill us with the Living Water.

Angel on Assignment

24 x 48    Acrylic

On Wednesday, driving home across the reservoir, I looked up to see a huge angel cloud before me over our hometown Canton. Saturday morning, Missionary friends visited us. That afternoon, I was awakened from a nap with the Lord saying, "Go paint that angel cloud now!" I painted, listening to guidance from Holy Spirit. Suddenly, a brilliant pure white light entered and only hit the head of the angel on the painting. This was a confirmation to me from God.

The next few days, three small earthquakes hit Canton.

Durable Refuge

18x24    Watercolor

The storm has passed by the strong barn used as a refuge over many generations. The sunlight streams in highlighting the barn and the colorful sycamore tree.

Granddaddy's Story

18 x 24     Watercolor

A red barn in the snow with geese flying against a golden sky.  The barn was located at intersection of Highway 43 and Dinkins Street in Canton, Mississippi.  The geese are in process of changing the lead.  I love to save the memories of barns.

Cloud of Blessing

16 x 20    Watercolor and Acrylic

I went outside to see the unusual color in the sky. I saw a blue, blue sky with only one huge pink cloud over our home which represents an anointing for our home and land. We give God the glory and thanksgiving.

Law and Order

22 ½ x 29 ½ Acrylic and Magic Marker

God's gift is supernatural design in snowflakes. Each one is unique. In October it started snowing at home and there was no wind blowing. I saw cascading out of the sky big individual snowflakes as if on plastic sheeting in perfect hexagon designs. Each snowflake was hexagon design and in a hexagon pattern. As I looked into the distance, the snowflakes became smaller and smaller but still fell in the hexagon pattern in perspective. A gentle wind came swirling the snowflakes which afterwards returned to the original pattern. Awesome!

The Marriage

18 x 24   Watercolor

I love this painting and the story behind it.  In marriage, we go through many ages and stages.

One day, the puffed-up male was very angry, pouring out his frustrations on the submissive, fiery orange bird.  The painting developed as in prayer the heavenly hosts appeared at the top, communicating with each other over the strained relationship.  Later, the dove of the Holy Spirit appeared extending a ring of unity and oneness for the future.

Colorful Gazing Garden Balls

18x24　　　Watercolor

I was at a garden nursery and saw the beautifully colored gazing balls in the window with sunlight pouring in and reflections making abstract designs on them. The pottery in the sunlight was creating light and shadows. In contrast to the bright and colorful gazing balls is the pastel landscape beyond the window.

Liquid Gold and Silvery Galaxy

48 x 48    Acrylic

I was sleeping and the Holy Spirit took me up into the heavenlies past numerous stars and galaxies. I was moving faster than the speed of light. I hung in the darkness feeling safe looking into the deep expanse below me and saw a vast, glorious and awesome spinning galaxy of pure liquid silver and pure liquid gold within the galaxy God is still creating.

This painting represents the Glory of God.

John the Baptist

36 x 72        Oil

God had given me an assignment to paint John the Baptist. Following the guidance to visit Israel and experience the people and land where he and Jesus walked, the vision of John the Baptist in the desert in front of a warm fire flowed onto the canvas.

John the Baptist
Close-up.

Jesus Christ, Great High Priest

40 x 40 Oil

The painting grew from the image of Jesus as a baby to reveal the power of His creating all universes. He is our great High Priest as depicted by the Jewish High Priest's jeweled breastplate representing the 12 tribes of Israel as in Exodus 28:15-30.

Jesus, Our Sacrifice

48 x 60    Oil

I had a burning desire to paint Jesus. He was in terrible pain carrying the heavy wooden cross to Calvary. I could not paint it until the Lord gave me a very meaningful trip to Israel.

When I returned, I was led to paint Jesus passing a window. The viewers thought they could watch and not get involved until He looked straight into their eyes. They were never the same.

Jesus, Our Sacrifice

Oil

The Holy Spirit of Jesus Christ

30 x 40　　　　　　　Watercolor and Pen

Kneeling in prayer and worshipping the Lord I sat back in my chair reading the scriptures. Suddenly, the room went gold and I saw the vision of a man far away coming closer and closer. I spoke the scripture of I John 4:1-3, knowing that Satan can come as an angel of light testing the spirit in this vision. As He approached smiling, I felt His overwhelming love and began to laugh and cry and was filled with the gift of joy. This gift has remained with me through the years.

The Key of David

18 x 24     Watercolor

Revelation 3:7 (Jesus said) "These are the words of Him who is holy and true, who holds the key of David – what he opens no one can shut; and what he shuts, no one can open. I know your deeds. See I have placed before you an open door that no one can shut. I know you have little strength, yet you have kept my word and have not denied my name."

Jesus could have denied the cross and crucifixion. He always had the key. We would have been lost in sin and forever separated from God the Father.

Now and Beyond – Dreams and Reality

18 x 24 Watercolor

Virginia Beach, Virginia – Artisan

18 x24       Watercolor

Beauty in the Ordinary

16 x 16   Watercolor

Beauty is where you find it!  Beautiful essence of the lights, shadows, and reflected light on the transparent layers of onion skins is challenging and intriguing.  Note the reflected numeral seven which is a holy number meaning perfection.  The Holy Spirit is present.

Petunias Galore

16x16   Watercolor

Painting of multiple-colored petunias in purples, blues, hot pink and white in sunlight with colorful shadows.

Exquisite Masterpiece

16 x 20   Oil Pencil

Oil pencil detailed study of the mature magnolia seedpod and leaves.  So exquisite!

Rufous-Sided Towhee

12 ½ x 19 ½     Watercolor

This is a painting of the black, white and rust male and the brown, cream and rust female together.

Birds in the Snow

24 x 30     Oil

This painting is of birds in the snow. The contrast and colors against the brilliant white is beautiful. Note the hidden birds.

The Gift of the Holy Spirit

13 ½ x 16 1/2     Acrylic

The snow-white dove appeared in the yard and rested, blessing me with the gift of the Holy Spirit. Why me? So peaceful and such a gift!

Covenant

14 x 18 1/2     Watercolor

The relationship in a covenant is lasting through trials as well as good times.

Golden Eagle

8 ½ x 11    Ink

Unconditional Love

15 x 19    Watercolor

I awoke laughing, seeing a precious, beautiful panda bear baby on green grass.  You know how it is to kiss a baby's tummy and the baby chortles out loud in a deep belly laugh?  It was a delightful way to awake – feeling unconditional love.

## Message in Lions

### 48 x 60    Oil

I walked into my house in this dream and was confronted by a huge, beautiful and muscular male lion. I said to him, "What are you doing in my house? This is my house!" He moved towards me and I quickly put up a 4 x 8 sheet of plywood over the door between us. He went through the wall into the next room and became a younger lion.

On my right, a huge female lion came beside me. I had no fear and reached out and comfortably rubbed her around her ears.

A psychiatrist friend said the male lions symbolized my father and husband and the female a symbol of my being comfortable with my femininity. A pastor said very confidently the male lions represent the Father and the Son and the female represents the Holy Spirit.

## When The Two Are One

48 x 60    Oil

A vision came of a wall of dirt. Two beautiful tigers emerged with their heads and front paws exposed. While watching them flex their paws in the sunlight, contented in their environment, they slowly disappeared back into the wall. The meaning of the vision was revealed that two different individuals can become one in spirit. Opposites attract.

## What Am I Not Seeing

48 x 48     Oil

Flying over the Pacific Ocean, I observed that the waves resembled wrinkled elephant skin. Over time at the beach, I saw the waves washing onto the shore and the wind rippling the dry sands with the same design. Tree bark, birds' legs, fish and turtle skin have a similar pattern. In photographs of mountains, clouds in the sky and older people's skin, textures are the same.

The name of the painting is "God Made the Moon and God Made Me and WHAT AM I NOT SEEING."

We live in a world with hidden mysteries, gifts, miracles, surprises and answers every day.

WHAT ARE WE NOT SEEING?

Random Choice

24x30    Oil

Visiting at the rodeo in the late afternoon, the bucking horses were in a holding pen with 2" round strong iron pipes. The late afternoon sun played across their bodies making shadows, lights, darks and midtones. The shadows of the horses against each other added to the composition. It was challenging to paint the Pinto who was white, brown and black as the designs played across its body. The effect was intriguing.

## Mixed Signals

24x32    Oil

Visiting the rodeo late in the day, the warm afternoon sun beat down upon the strong iron pipes of the pen where the awaiting bucking bulls were held. I was intrigued with the shadows, which made patterns play across their bodies.

## Nearing the End

### 18x24   Watercolor

A farmer is plowing in the field behind two large percherons in the late afternoon completing the short rows. A bluebird sits at his fencepost nest watching the farmer. The intricate treatment of the shrimp, pink and cream peace roses shows clarity. The colors of the roses are repeated in the sky and background. The rift in the sky was healed by the covering of the oncoming clouds.

## Backs to the Wind

18 x 24    Watercolor

Before we built the barn, the horses were subject to the elements.

We had a sudden snow after rain and sleet. The wind was whistling and they stood with their backs to the wind, their tails covered in icicles.

Southern Lady With Wisteria

18 x 24   Watercolor

This is a painting of a stately antebellum home with flowing wisteria taking us back to the past.

Ride Into the Darkness With Love

36 x 48     Oil

I was awakened by a vision of a dark-haired lady with a black lace shawl, black dress and black boots on a black horse. She was looking off into the distance with confidence and yet her heart was disillusioned with unrealistic expectations looking within. The dream vision reveals moving into a new, more complete emotional and spiritual journey.

## Katie

23 x 30                Mixed Medium

Katie depicts the woman in the painting "Ride Into the Darkness With Love" shedding her dark life and blossoming into spiritual richness and fulfillment.
A mistake is an opportunity to be creative. The painting happened as I painted "Ride Into the Darkness With Love" – the watercolor of Katie fell into the oil pallet. I scraped off the blobs of paint and later decided I could repair it by making flowers out of the blobs, added the lace with watercolor and doilies to make the lace.

Mr. Eric Larson Turner

14 x 16     Oil

Portrait of Mr. Eric Larson Turner. Memories of a friend's grandfather depicted in antique glazes.

Michael and Kitten

36 x 48        Oil

A dear relationship between a boy and his kitten, Tiger.

Allison Grogan Wedding Day

24 x 26          Oil

The painting is a portrait of a southern bride. The tulle riding veil and the antique cotton lace wedding dress were quite challenging to capture. Her beauty is the essence of a strong, talented and gentle woman.

## Contemplation

13 ½ x 17 ½    Watercolor

In the Church, the morning light was pouring in over an older gentleman praying. His white hair glistened in the sunlight. I was very moved to capture his contemplation. I chose watercolor leaving the white paper for his hair and the highlights. The painting was achieved by using two colors of blues and orange.

The painting reveals his intimate moment with the Lord Jesus.

Stages of Enlightenment

18 x 24  Watercolor

The young dove is mirrored in the water seeking to find out who he is.  The male dove is coming to court the female.  Just as the doves, we live life maturing and growing spiritually.  The Holy Spirit, white dove in the background, is present throughout all stages.

# EARLY MORNING ADDITION ACKKNOWLEDGEMENTS

Who are we that the ONE and ONLY LORD GOD cares for us, shares our thoughts, words, and decisions? THIS AWESOME BEING not only knows how many hairs we have, sparrows there are, but how many molecules, atoms, stars, planets, and galaxies exist.

Who are we to judge this AWESOME GOD, but we do. HE says that we cannot understand HIS ways.

We who are limited in our vision, hearing, and understanding, don't even see like other beings. The bees see flowers in different patterns, spiders see with many eyes, some animals see only black, white, and shades of grey. Have you heard of photography that can see jets of energy from fingers and even leaves?

How big is your God? Are you your god? Does your intellectual prowess demand superiority over others of very different brains? These "different" brains know things you never even thought.

How big is your God? Do you realize microwaves, radio waves, and many different others are flowing through your body every minute? Understand there are zillions of unrealized, undiscovered, miracles yet to be "invented." They already exist but humans have killed the babies who were to be open enough to the HOLY SPIRIT, who reveals these miracles and inventions through revelations.

How big is your God? What if UFOs are very real and superior to our limited understanding? Does that make God smaller or (what is the largest word to describe anything or anyone)?

Our GOD, YAWH, JEHOVAH, ADONAI has revealed HIMSELF to us humans, through His SON, JESUS CHRIST, to know HIM as the ONE and ONLY GOD of LOVE, who is SPIRIT. WE are flesh and spirit, made in HIS image, created by HIM. This is my GOD. This is the GOD of SPIRIT FILLED BORN AGAIN CHRISTIANS who have surrendered to the GIFT from GOD, HIS SON JESUS CHRIST.

We are never alone. Our journey is never unguided. We are always silently, sometimes audibly counseled and guided by HIM. My life has always, even as a young child through the teachings of my precious mother and grandparents, been in relationship with HIM, as FATHER, JESUS, then HOLY SPIRIT.

My walk has been learning to grow in prayer, scripture, listening, hearing, and obeying, as has your spiritual journey.

How can I use words to express the intimate walk, the consuming SPIRIT indwelling with my spirit? Accepting JESUS CHRIST AS LORD AND SAVIOR.

My journey is expressed through the God given artistic gift of drawing and painting; never alone.

# Perry T. Ritchie Biography

Perry T. Ritchie began drawing as a child in Laurel, Mississippi. She attended Mississippi State College for Women and received a BA in Education from the University of Mississippi. She is married to Jim Ritchie, author and storyteller, and has three children – Jim, Anne and Rick and numerous grandchildren.

She has studied with many of the country's best-known artists and continues to take classes to refine her skills. "Using our gifts and talents to glorify God, we have a responsibility to share our talent and knowledge with others."

The artist believes that keeping balance in life through love of God, family, friends, nature and self is important. She also feels that each person should have an interest that is both nourishing and rewarding.

Perry's diversity in subject matter includes wild and domestic animals, florals, landscapes, portraits, dreams as they relate to life's spiritual journey and biblical scenes. Her mastery of media is immense: she is an extremely prolific artist. Her deep respect for life is evident in each of her paintings.

She has shown her paintings in numerous individual and group shows as well as competitions. Collectors of her work number in the hundreds, and some of her patrons own whole series of paintings. Perry teaches drawing and painting in watercolor and oil. The artist welcomes commissions.

Illustrations by Perry Thickens Ritchie:

Shocco Tales Southern Fried Sagas by Jim Ritchie
Shocco Tales Shavin's Under a Southern Shade Tree by Jim Ritchie
A Heart's Desire by Virginia Alford
What Am I Not Seeing written and illustrated by Perry Ritchie
Visions of Redemption in a Fallen World written and illustrated by Perry Ritchie

Her work can be seen at Shocco Studio and Retreat Center, 708 Ratliff Ferry Road, Canton, MS 39046. Contact by E-mail: perryritchie@bellsouth.net

www.ingramcontent.com/pod-product-compliance
Lightning Source LLC
Chambersburg PA
CBHW061109070526
44579CB00012B/189